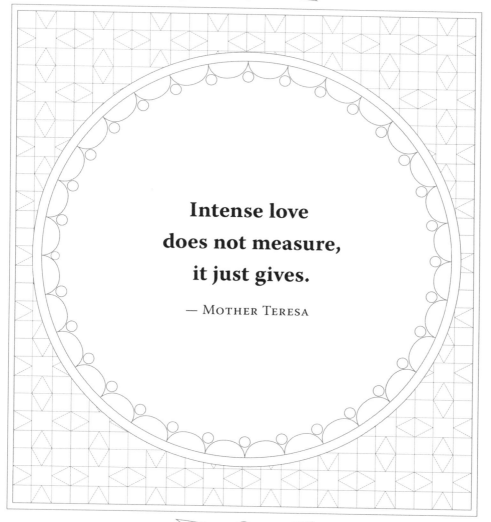

**Intense love
does not measure,
it just gives.**

— MOTHER TERESA

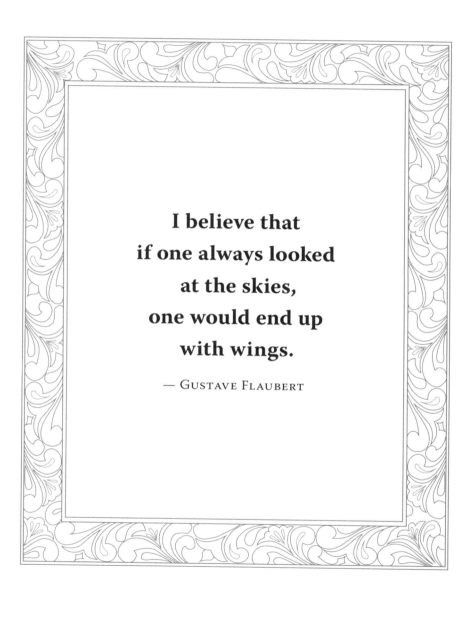

I believe that
if one always looked
at the skies,
one would end up
with wings.

— GUSTAVE FLAUBERT

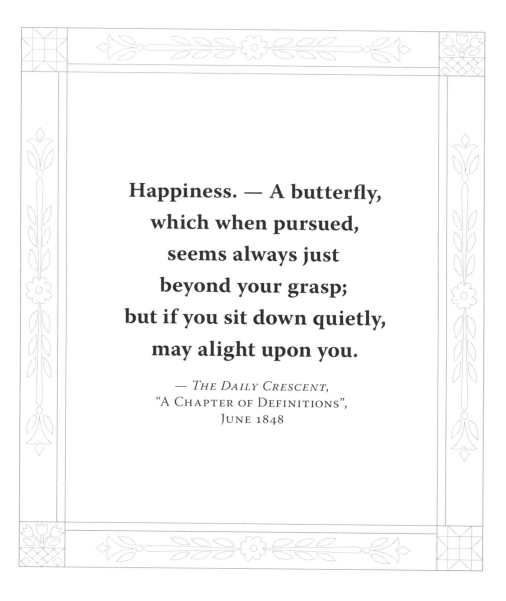

Happiness. — A butterfly,
which when pursued,
seems always just
beyond your grasp;
but if you sit down quietly,
may alight upon you.

— *The Daily Crescent*,
"A Chapter of Definitions",
June 1848

**All you need is love.
But a little chocolate
now and then
doesn't hurt.**

— CHARLES SCHULZ

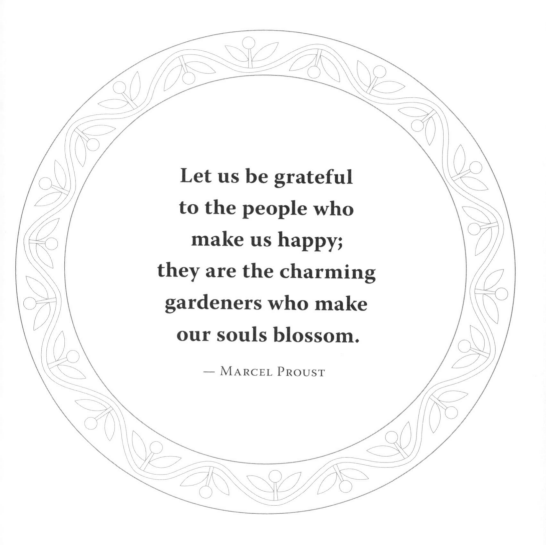

Let us be grateful
to the people who
make us happy;
they are the charming
gardeners who make
our souls blossom.

— MARCEL PROUST

It didn't matter how big our house was; it mattered that there was love in it.

— PETER BUFFETT,
LIFE IS WHAT YOU MAKE IT

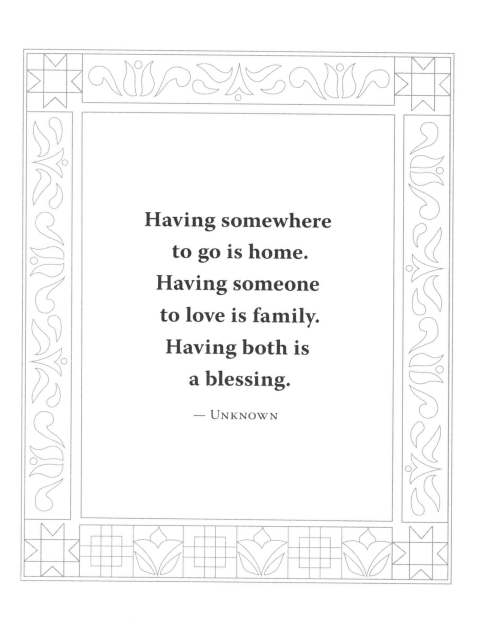

Having somewhere
to go is home.
Having someone
to love is family.
Having both is
a blessing.

— UNKNOWN

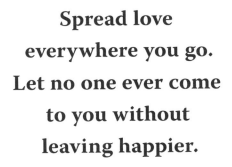

**Spread love
everywhere you go.
Let no one ever come
to you without
leaving happier.**

— Mother Teresa

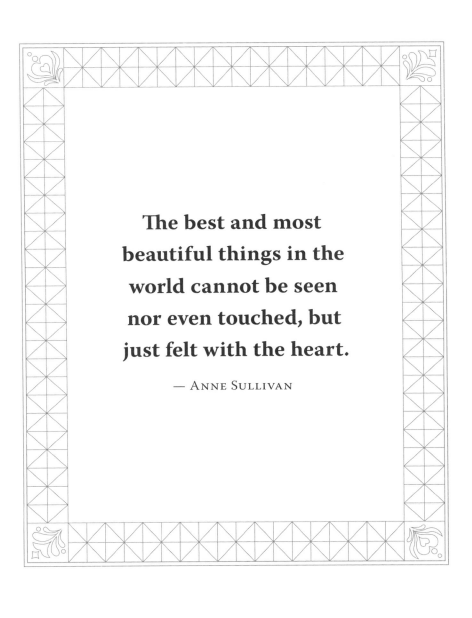

The best and most
beautiful things in the
world cannot be seen
nor even touched, but
just felt with the heart.

— ANNE SULLIVAN

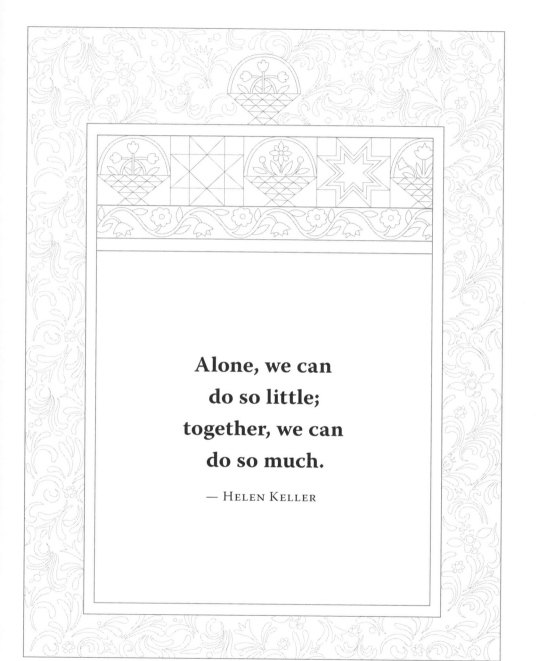

**Alone, we can
do so little;
together, we can
do so much.**

— Helen Keller

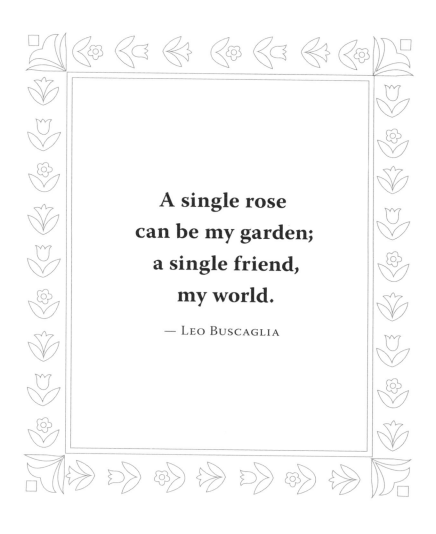

**A single rose
can be my garden;
a single friend,
my world.**

— LEO BUSCAGLIA

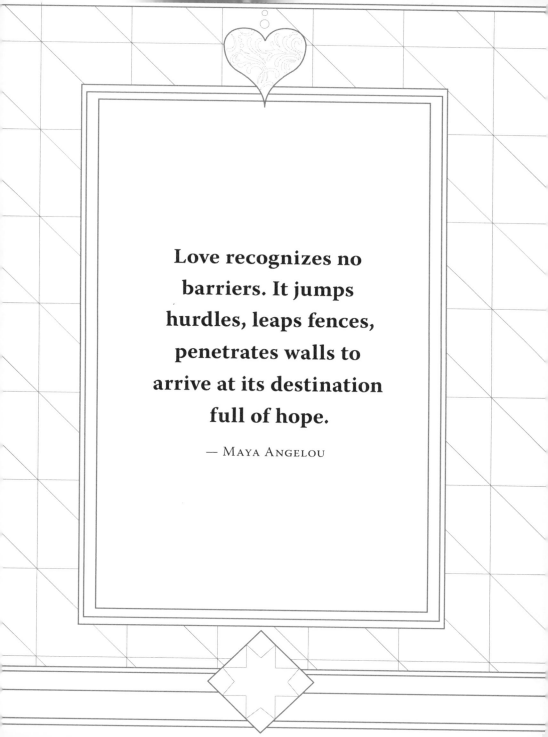

Love recognizes no barriers. It jumps hurdles, leaps fences, penetrates walls to arrive at its destination full of hope.

— MAYA ANGELOU

About Jim Shore

Jim Shore grew up in rural South Carolina, the son of artistic parents who instilled a love of American folk art. His grandmother was a master quilter who taught him the patience and skill to bring intricate designs to life. Jim worked for decades developing his craft, manufacturing his own designs, and traveling the country to sell his work. Finally, in 2001, he partnered with Enesco to create Heartwood Creek, the successful brand that brought Jim worldwide fame. Jim has received multiple awards from prestigious trade organizations, including the ICON

HONORS Life Accomplishment Award in 2012. Through his partnership with Enesco, the Jim Shore Collection has grown from a small group of Santas, snowmen, and angels to a broad year-round brand respected and sold around the world. Jim's boundless creativity and unique ability enable him to touch people in all walks of life through his art.

ISBN 978-1-64178-121-3

Fox Chapel Publishing makes every effort to use environmentally friendly paper for printing.

© 2021 by Jim Shore and Quiet Fox Designs, *www.QuietFoxDesigns.com*, an imprint of Fox Chapel Publishing Company, Inc., 903 Square Street, Mount Joy, PA 17552.

We are always looking for talented authors and artists. To submit an idea, please send a brief inquiry to acquisitions@foxchapelpublishing.com.

Printed in Singapore
First printing